1911 manual fire engine

1870 horse-drawn steam fire engine

ladders (four types)   hose locker   oxygen cylinders   water and foam tanks

water pump

small hose reel

A modern multi-purpose fire fighting vehicle

to teachers and parents

This is a LADYBIRD LEADER book, one of a series specially produced to meet the very real need for carefully planned *first information books* that instantly attract enquiring minds and stimulate reluctant readers.

The subject matter and vocabulary have been selected with expert assistance, and the brief and simple text is printed in large, clear type.

Children's questions are anticipated and facts presented in a logical sequence. Where possible, the books show what happened in the past and what is relevant today.

Special artwork has been commissioned to set a standard rarely seen in books for this reading age and at this price.

Full colour illustrations are on all 48 pages to give maximum impact and provide the extra enrichment that is the aim of all Ladybird Leaders.

The publishers would like to thank Station Officer Cook, G.I. Fire E. of Leicestershire Fire Service for his valuable help.

A Ladybird Leader

fire

by James Webster
with illustrations by Frank Humphris

Ladybird Books Ltd Loughborough 1977

The greatest fire of all

The sun is a ball of fire.
It gives us light and heat.
Without this great fire,
there would be no life on Earth.

Nature's fires

When men first saw fire,
they were afraid.

Later, they learned to make
and use it.

When lightning flashed,
they thought the gods were angry.

See what happens

Keep rubbing your hands together.
What do you feel?

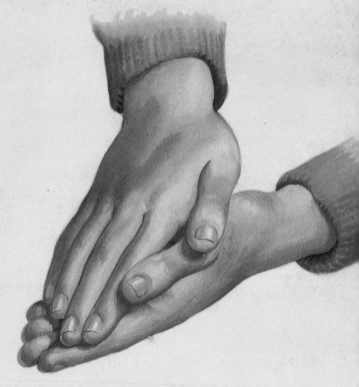

Making fire

Rubbing makes things hot.
Stone Age men first made fire
by rubbing one piece of wood
against another.

Fire was needed for many things

To keep warm and dry.

To keep away wild animals.

To cook food.

To harden clay pots.

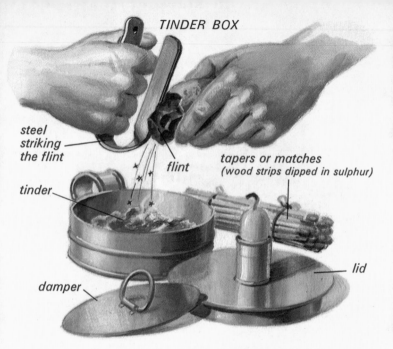

TINDER BOX

steel striking the flint

flint

tapers or matches
(wood strips dipped in sulphur)

tinder

lid

damper

The flint is struck with the steel—sparks fall into the *tinder*
(very dry material which is easily set alight)—
the tinder is gently blown until it glows— then the taper
is lit from the glowing tinder.
The damper is used to snuff or put out the tinder.

Other ways of making fire

As time went on, men found
that when flint and steel
were struck together,
they gave off sparks.
(*Flint* is a kind of stone.)

Then men found even easier ways to make fire.

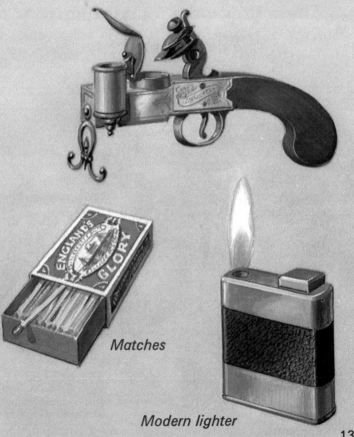

Mechanical tinder lighter
The flint, held in the hammer, struck
the steel when the trigger was pulled
and the sparks showered into the tinder.

Matches

Modern lighter

One fire for everything

The first huts had a fire
in the middle.

The roof had a hole above the fire
to let the smoke out.

These fires were for cooking,
and warmth, and light.

Fire worship

For a long time
men thought fire was a god,
and they worshipped it.

Even today fire worship
is part of some religions.

15

Fuels used for fires

Many fuels are used for fires,
including coal, wood, paraffin
and many gases.

Here a man cuts peat
to heat his cottage.

Peat has to dry
before it will burn well.

Fire helps health

Even long ago, men knew
that hot baths
helped crippled people
and those with skin diseases.

Fire used as light

Fire gives light as well as heat.
Early men used oil lamps
to light their caves.

Two hundred years ago
there were no street lamps
even in the cities.

In England, it was safer to go out
with a boy who led the way
with a flaming torch.

Fire and metals

When men found
that fire melted metal,
they could shape it
to make tools and weapons.

Since that time,
men have been trying to build
hotter and hotter furnaces
to melt or make all kinds of things.

Fire as a tool

Man has found
that fire can be used
to work for him.

It can weld metals together.

It can kill weeds.

It can burn off old paint.

Sending messages by fire

In times of danger,
big bonfires called beacons
were lit to give warning
across the country.

Red Indians also used fire
to send messages.
They made big puffs of smoke
which could be seen far away.

Smoke from fires

Not long ago,
many towns were like this.

Coal fires made a lot of smoke.

Today towns are much cleaner
when heated by gas,
oil and electricity.

Smoke can kill

Less than thirty years ago,
some people died from breathing
smoky, foggy air (called *smog*)
and many people were ill.

Laws have been passed
all over the world
to clear the air of smoke.

People can die
from smoking
cigarettes.

See what happens

Ask a grown-up
to light
a short candle.

Now, cover it
with a jam jar.
What happens?

Fire needs air

This bonfire is going out.
It is not getting
much air.

This bonfire is burning well,
because it is being given
lots of air.

Fire as a weapon

At one time,
old ships were filled with tar,
and set on fire.

They were blown by the wind
towards the enemy
and burnt his ships.

Red Indians
sometimes fired
flame-tipped arrows
at their enemies.

Nowadays bombs
can turn a town
into one huge fire.

Fireworks are fun —
but dangerous!

Every year on Guy Fawkes night,
many children are killed
or injured.

Fireworks are dangerous
to play with.

A firework display
run by your school
or Community Centre
can be very beautiful and exciting.

There are many more fireworks
than you could have at home.

Instead of being dangerous,
it is great fun, and lasts longer
than your own fireworks would.

Power from fire

Fire turns water to steam.
This was used to drive
the first engines.

*Engines like this
pumped water
out of deep coal
mines*

For 150 years, most trains
were pulled by steam locomotives.

One man drove the train.

Another man, called the fireman,
stoked the fire.

Power from fire

For some time,
ships had both steam engines
and sails.

Men called stokers
looked after the fires in ships.

Fire warms the air in this balloon.

The warm air rises
and takes the balloon up.

The flame behind a space ship
is burning gas.

This kind of fire
drives all the big rockets.

Fire is dangerous

When houses are built of wood,
fire is a great danger.

Nearly half
of London's wooden buildings
were burnt down in 1666.

Fire from volcanoes

The rich lower slopes of volcanoes
are good for growing food.

Men have even built towns
near volcanoes because of this.

Pompeii, a town near the foot
of Mount Vesuvius,
was destroyed 2000 years ago.

Even as recently as 1961,
people were killed and their homes
were destroyed by volcanic eruption
on the island of Tristan da Cunha
in the south Atlantic Ocean.

How the sun's rays can start a fire

A forest fire

Forest fires are often started through carelessness with matches, cigarettes, and broken glass.

How to prevent fire

Worn flexes, old electric blankets
and overloaded plugs
can all cause fires.
Have them checked!

Cigarette ends left burning
are particularly dangerous.
See they are stubbed out.

This should never happen—all fires must be guarded

At night,
remove all electric plugs,
shut all doors,
and put fire guards
in front of any open fires.

If fire breaks out (in Britain)

Warn anyone in the building.
Dial 999 and ask for the Fire Brigade.

Wait and answer all the questions.

If you are trapped on the first floor by fire

1

Put blankets at bottom of door to keep out smoke.

2

Open window and shout for help.
WHEREVER YOU LIVE IN THE WORLD, FIND OUT WHAT
YOU SHOULD DO IN CASE OF FIRE.

3

If the heat or smoke
become unbearable,
drop all the soft material
you can find
out of the window
onto the ground below
to break your fall.

4

Get out onto window sill,

5

turn round,

6

lower yourself carefully
to the full length
of your arms.
You are now
much nearer the ground.

7

Let go and drop.

Fighting fire

Here is the way
a British fire station might deal
with a call to a fire like this:

10.13 Fire at Edwards Furniture, 18 High Street, Reedbury, reported by telephone.

10.14 Water Tender and Pump Escape sent, Station Officer informed by radio telephone in his car.

10.16 Police and Water Authority informed.

10.19 Water Tender and Pump Escape arrive at fire.

10.21 Station Officer asks for two more Water Tenders, Turntable Ladder, and breathing apparatus.

10.22 Water Tender and Turntable Ladder leave Woodville Fire Station. Water Tender leaves Haston Fire Station.

10.28 Message from Divisional Officer at fire: "A furniture shop of two and three floors about 40 by 100 ft, well alight on ground and first floor, difficult access to boundaries."

10.30 Water Tender from Haston arrives.

10.32 Water Tender and Turntable Ladder from Woodville arrive.

10.36 Stop message (means no further assistance required) from Divisional Officer. "Furniture shop severely damaged by fire, six water jets and Turntable Ladder in use from four street hydrants."

10.40	Salvage Tender requested.
10.41	Salvage Tender sent from Essenvale Fire Station.
11.15	Woodville and Haston Water Tenders and Turntable Ladder return to their home stations.
11.17	Salvage Tender arrives.
11.45	Pump Escape returns to Reedbury.
12.06	Water Tender returns to Reedbury.
15.00	Fire-damaged shop re-inspected to make sure fire is completely out.
18.15	Final inspection is made — no further inspections deemed necessary.

Skylab *with its solar panels extended is powered by energy from the sun*

How the sun's fire helps man

When man works in space,
his energy supply
comes from the sun.

Index

	page
Air	31, 39
Atlantic Ocean	42
Balloon	39
Beacons	24
Bonfires	24, 31
Candle experiment	30
Cigarettes	29, 43, 44
Clay pots	11
Coal	16, 26
Coal mines	36
Defence	10
Dwellings	14, 18
Electricity	27
Fire :	
and metals	20
as a tool	22, 23
as light	4, 14, 18, 19
fighting	front endpaper, 48, 49, 50
if fire breaks out	46, 47
making fire	9, 12, 13
power from fire	36, 37, 38, 39
prevention	44, 45
uses	10, 11, 14
worship	15
Fireworks	34, 35
Flint	12, 13
Forest fires	43
Fuels	16
Furnaces	21
Gas	27, 39
Guy Fawkes	34
Laws on smoke	28
Lighter, modern	13
Matches	12, 13, 43
Oil	27
Oil lamps	18
Paraffin	16
Peat	16
Pompeii	42
Red Indians	25, 33
Religion	7, 15
Rockets	39
Sending messages	24, 25
Ships	38
Skylab	51
Smog	28
Smoke	26, 28
Solar energy	51
Space	51
Space ship	39
Steam	36, 37, 38
Steel	12, 13
Stokers	38
Stone Age	9
Sun	4, 51
Tapers	12
Tinder box	12
Tinder lighter	13
Tools	20, 22, 23
Trains	37
Tristan da Cunha	42
Vesuvius, Mount	42
Volcanoes	6, 42